Merry Christmas Carols

20 best loved carols to play and sing

Arranged for easy piano by

Fanny Waterman

Faber Music Limited

London

At Christmas time everyone wants to play and sing carols.

This collection has been specially compiled to enable the pianist of modest ability to perform some of the best loved carols and Christmas songs. The arrangements give scope for many attractive pianistic effects, and are equally suitable as accompaniments to carol singing. While they are well within the grasp of young pianists, they will also appeal to players of all ages for use in the home, school and elsewhere.

Merry Christmas Carols will, in fact, give every pianist the opportunity of making a real contribution to the enjoyment of the festive season.

F.W.

Arrangements © 1986 by Faber Music Ltd
First published in 1986 by Faber Music Ltd
3 Queen Square London WC1N 3AU
Music drawn by Lincoln Castle Music
Cover illustration by Jill Bennett
Cover designed by M & S Tucker
Printed in England by Halstan & Co Ltd

CONTENTS

	Page
Away in a Manger (2 tunes)	8,9
Deck the Hall	19
Ding Dong Merrily on High	18
God Rest you Merry Gentlemen	4
Good King Wenceslas	5
Hark! the Herald Angels Sing	17
In dulci jubilo	13
I Saw Three Ships (2 tunes)	7
Jingle Bells	20
O Come, All ye Faithful (Duet)	26,27
O Little Town of Bethlehem (2 tunes)	14,15
Once in Royal David's City	12
Rocking (Duet)	24,25
See, amid the Winter's Snow (Duet)	22,23
Silent Night	11
The First Noel	10
The Holly and the Ivy	6
We Three Kings	16
We Wish you a Merry Christmas	28
While Shepherds Watched	12

4

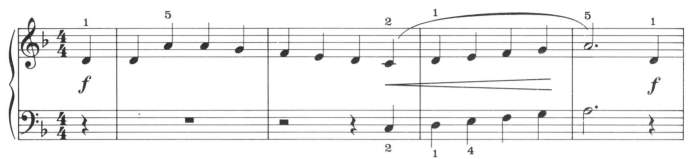

God Rest you Merry Gentlemen

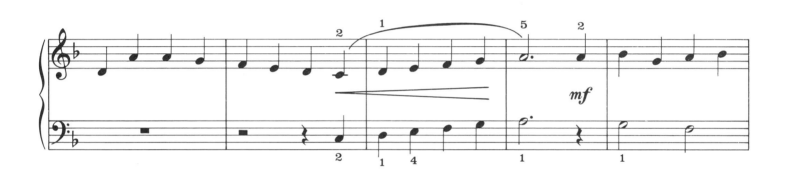

Chorus

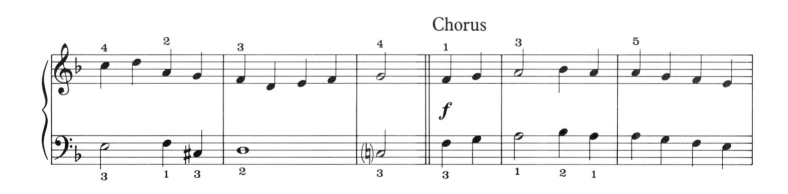

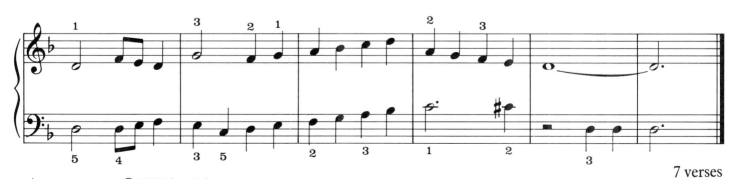

7 verses

Good King Wenceslas

5 verses

The Holly and the Ivy

Chorus

6 verses

I Saw Three Ships

First Tune

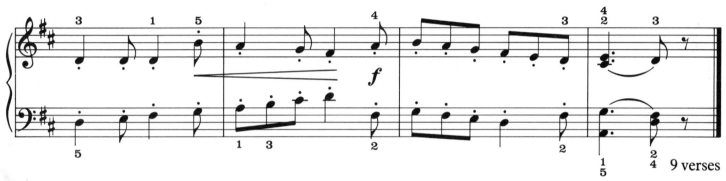

9 verses

I Saw Three Ships

Second Tune

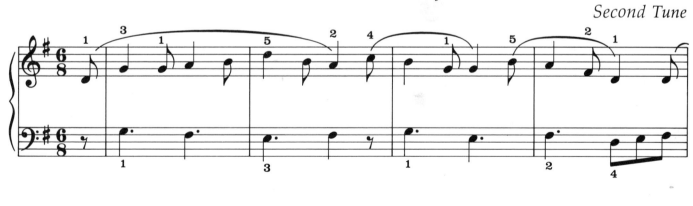

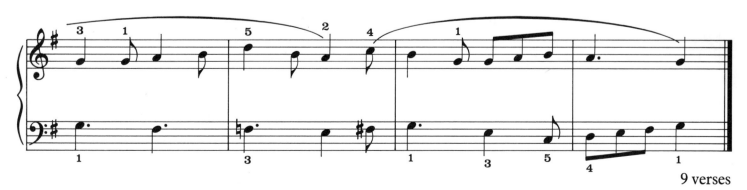

9 verses

Away in a Manger

English Tune

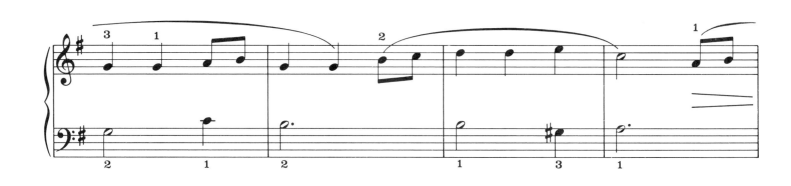

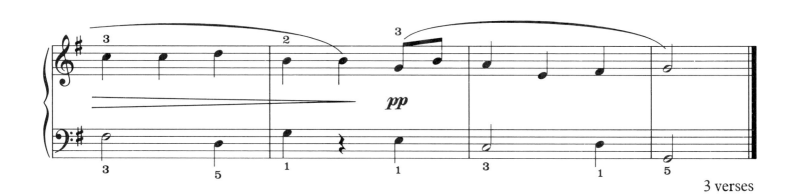

3 verses

Away in a Manger

American Tune

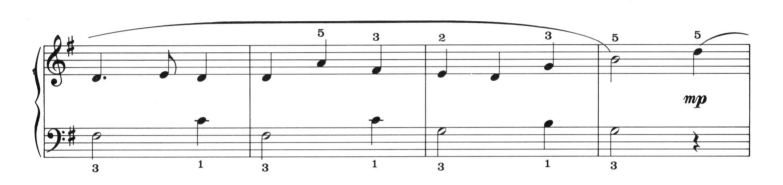

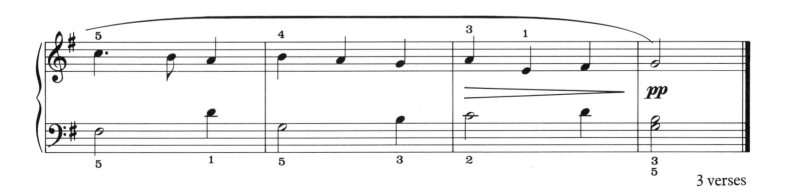

3 verses

The First Noel

Chorus

6 verses

Silent Night

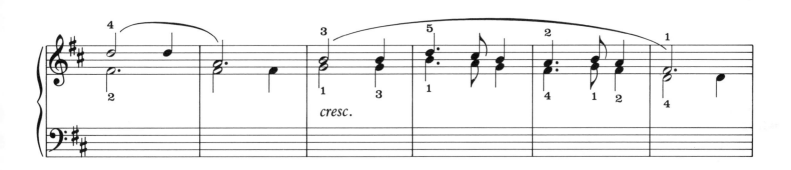

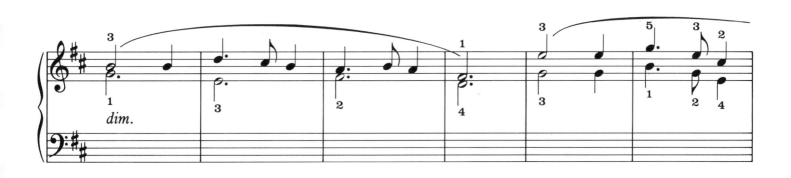

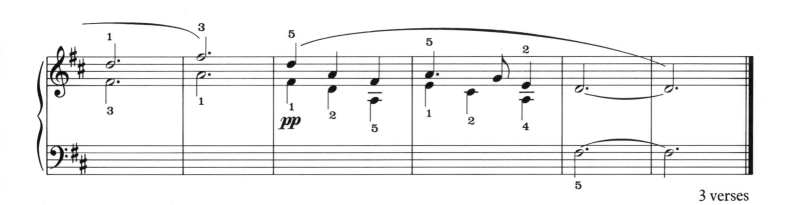

3 verses

While Shepherds Watched

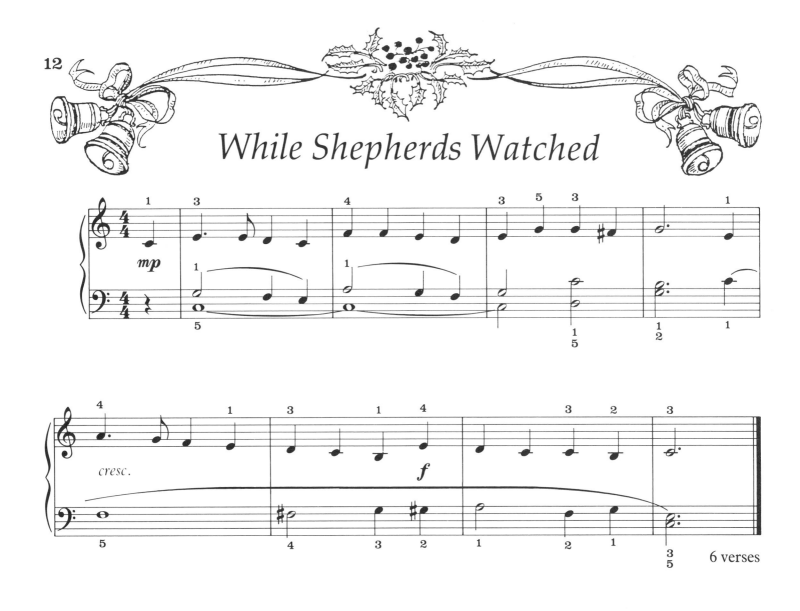

6 verses

Once in Royal David's City

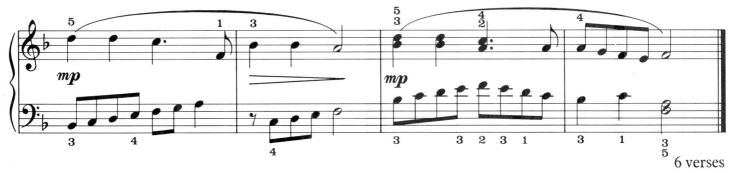

6 verses

In dulci jubilo

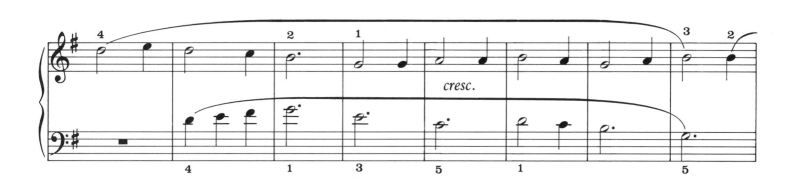

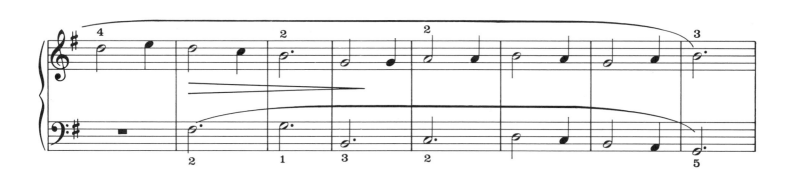

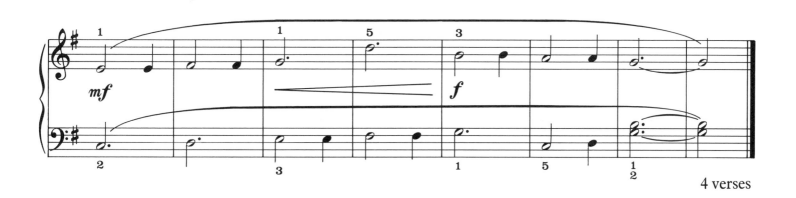

4 verses

O Little Town of Bethlehem

English Tune

4 verses

Merry Christmas Carols

God Rest you Merry Gentlemen

1. God rest you merry gentlemen,
   Let nothing you dismay.
   Remember Christ our Saviour
   Was born on Christmas day,
   To save our souls from Satan's power
   When we had gone astray:
   O tidings of comfort and joy,
   Comfort and joy,
   O tidings of comfort and joy.

2. In Bethlehem in Jewry
   This blessed Babe was born,
   And laid within a manger
   Upon this blessed morn,
   The which his Mother Mary
   Did nothing take in scorn:
   O tidings, etc.

3. From God our heavenly Father
   A blessed angel came,
   And unto certain shepherds
   Brought tidings of the same,
   How that in Bethlehem was born
   The Son of God by name:
   O tidings, etc.

4. 'Fear not' then said the angel,
   'Let nothing you affright;
   This day is born a Saviour
   Unto a Virgin bright
   To free all you who trust in him
   From Satan's power and might:'
   O tidings, etc.

5. The shepherds at these tidings
   Rejoiced much in mind,
   And left their flocks a-feeding
   In tempest, storm, and wind,
   And went to Bethlehem staightway
   The Son of God to find:
   O tidings, etc.

6. Now when they came to Bethlehem
   Whereat the Infant lay,
   They found him in a manger
   Where oxen feed on hay;
   His Mother Mary kneeling down
   Unto the Lord did pray:
   O tidings, etc.

7. Now to the Lord sing praises
   All you within this place,
   And with true love and brotherhood
   Each other now embrace;
   This holy tide of Christmas
   All others doth deface:
   O tidings, etc.

Good King Wenceslas

1. Good King Wenceslas looked out,
   On the feast of Stephen,
   When the snow lay round about,
   Deep and crisp and even:
   Brightly shone the moon that night,
   Though the frost was cruel,
   When a poor man came in sight,
   Gath'ring winter fuel.

2. 'Hither page and stand by me,
   If thou knowest it, telling,
   Yonder peasant who is he?
   Where and what his dwelling?'
   'Sire, he lives a good league hence,
   Underneath the mountain,
   Right against the forest fence,
   By St. Agnes fountain.'

3. 'Bring me flesh and bring me wine,
   Bring me pine logs hither:
   Thou and I will see him dine,
   When we bear them thither.'
   Page and monarch, forth they went,
   Forth they went together;
   Through the rude wind's wild lament
   And the bitter weather.

4. 'Sire, the night is darker now,
   And the wind blows stronger;
   Fails my heart, I know not how;
   I can go no longer.'
   'Mark my footsteps, good my page;
   Tread thou in them boldly:
   Thou shalt find the winter's rage
   Freeze thy blood less coldly.'

5. In his master's steps he trod,
   Where the snow lay dinted;
   Heat was in the very sod
   Which the saint had printed.
   Therefore, Christian men, be sure,
   Wealth or rank possessing,
   You who now will bless the poor,
   Shall yourselves find blessing.

The Holly and the Ivy

1. The holly and the ivy,
   When they are both full grown,
   Of all the trees that are in the wood,
   The holly bears the crown:
   The rising of the sun
   And the running of the deer,
   The playing of the merry organ,
   Sweet singing in the choir.

The holly and the ivy (cont.)

2. The holly bears a blossom,
   As white as the lily flower,
   And Mary bore sweet Jesus Christ
   To be our sweet Saviour:
   The rising of the sun, etc.

3. The holly bears a berry,
   As red as any blood,
   And Mary bore sweet Jesus Christ
   To do poor sinners good:
   The rising of the sun, etc.

4. The holly bears a prickle,
   As sharp as any thorn,
   And Mary bore sweet Jesus Christ
   On Christmas day in the morn:
   The rising of the sun, etc.

5. The holly bears a bark,
   As bitter as any gall,
   And Mary bore sweet Jesus Christ
   For to redeem us all:
   The rising of the sun, etc.

6. The holly and the ivy,
   When they are both full grown,
   Of all the trees that are in the wood,
   The holly bears the crown:
   The rising of the sun, etc.

I Saw Three Ships

1. I saw three ships come sailing in,
   On Christmas Day, on Christmas Day,
   I saw three ships come sailing in
   On Christmas Day in the morning.

2. And what was in those ships all three?
   On Christmas Day, etc.

3. Our Saviour Christ and his lady.
   On Christmas Day, etc.

4. Pray, whither sailed those ships all three?
   On Christmas Day, etc.

5. O, they sailed into Bethlehem.
   On Christmas Day, etc.

6. And all the bells on earth shall ring.
   On Christmas Day, etc.

7. And all the angels in Heaven shall sing.
   On Christmas Day, etc.

8. And all the souls on earth shall sing.
   On Christmas Day, etc.

9. Then let us all rejoice amain!
   On Christmas Day, etc.

Away in a Manger

1. Away in a manger, no crib for a bed,
    The little Lord Jesus laid down his
                              sweet head.
   The stars in the bright sky looked down
                              where he lay,
   The little Lord Jesus asleep on the hay.

2. The cattle are lowing, the Baby awakes,
    But little Lord Jesus, no crying he makes.
   I love you, Lord Jesus, look down from the sky,
    And stay by my side till morning is nigh.

3. Be near me, Lord Jesus; I ask you to stay
    Close by me for ever, and love me, I pray.
   Bless all the dear children in your tender care,
    And fit us for heaven to live with you there.

The First Noel

1. The first Noel the Angel did say,
    Was to certain poor shepherds in fields
                              as they lay;
   In fields where they lay keeping their sheep,
    On a cold winter's night that was so deep:
   Noel, Noel, Noel, Noel,
   Born is the King of Israel.

2. They looked up and saw a star,
    Shining in the east, beyond them far,
   And to the earth it gave great light,
    And so it continued both day and night:
   Noel, etc.

3. And by the light of that same star,
    Three wise men came from country far;
   To seek for a King was their intent,
    And to follow the star wherever it went:
   Noel, etc.

4. This star drew nigh to the north-west,
    O'er Bethlehem it took its rest,
   And there it did both stop and stay,
    Right over the place where Jesus lay:
   Noel, etc.

5. Then entered in those Wise Men three,
    Full reverently upon their knee,
   And offered there in his presence,
    Their gold and myrrh and frankincense:
   Noel, etc.

6. Then let us all with one accord,
    Sing praises to our Heavenly Lord,
   That has made heaven and earth of nought,
    And with his blood mankind has bought:
   Noel, etc.

Silent Night

1. Silent night, Holy night,
    All is calm, all is bright;
   Round the Virgin Mother and Child,
    Holy infant so tender and mild,
   Sleep in heavenly peace,
    Sleep in heavenly peace.

2. Silent night, Holy night,
    Shepherds quake at the sight;
   Glories stream from heaven afar,
    Heavenly hosts sing Alleluya:
   Christ the Saviour is born,
    Christ the Saviour is born.

3. Silent night, Holy night,
    Son of God, love's pure light;
   Radiance beams from your holy face,
    With the dawn of redeeming grace;
   Jesus, Lord, at your birth,
    Jesus, Lord, at your birth.

Once in Royal David's City

1. Once in royal David's city
    Stood a lowly cattle shed,
   Where a mother laid her baby
    In a manger for his bed;
   Mary was that mother mild,
    Jesus Christ her little child.

2. He came down to earth from heaven
    Who is God and Lord of all,
   And his shelter was a stable,
    And his cradle was a stall;
   With the poor and mean and lowly
    Lived on earth our Saviour holy.

3. And through all his wondrous childhood
    He would honour and obey,
   Love and watch the lowly maiden,
    In whose gentle arms he lay;
   Christian children all must be
    Mild, obedient, good as he.

4. For he is our childhood's pattern,
    Day by day like us he grew,
   He was little, weak, and helpless,
    Tears and smiles like us he knew;
   And he feeleth for our sadness,
    And he shareth in our gladness.

5. And our eyes at last shall see him,
    Through his own redeeming love,
   For that child so dear and gentle
    Is our Lord in heaven above;
   And he leads his children on
    To the place where he is gone.

6. Not in that poor lowly stable,
    With the oxen standing by,
   We shall see him, but in heaven,
    Set at God's right hand on high;
   When like stars his children crowned
    All in white shall wait around.

In dulci jubilo

1. *In dulci jubilo*
   Let us our homage show;
   Our hearts' joy reclineth
   In præsepio,
   And like a bright star shineth
   Matris in gremio:
   Alpha es et O!

2. *O Jesu parvule!*
   My heart is sore for thee!
   Hear me, I beseech thee,
   O Puer optime!
   My prayer let it reach thee,
   O Princeps Gloriæ!
   Trahe me post Te!

3. *O Patris caritas!*
   O Nati lenitas!
   Deeply were we stained
   Per nostra crimina;
   But Thou hast for us gained
   Cælorum gaudia:
   O that we were there!

4. *Ubi sunt gaudia*
   If that they be not there?
   There are angels singing
   Nova cantica;
   There the bells are ringing
   In Regis curia:
   O that we were there!

While Shepherds Watched

1. While shepherds watched their flocks by night,
    All seated on the ground,
   The angel of the Lord came down
    And glory shone around.

2. 'Fear not,' said he: for mighty dread
    Had seized their troubled mind;
   'Glad tidings of great joy I bring
    To you and all mankind.

3. To you in David's town this day
    Is born of David's line
   A Saviour, who is Christ the Lord;
    And this shall be the sign:

4. The heavenly Babe you there shall find
    To human view displayed,
   All meanly wrapped in swathing bands,
    And in a manger laid.'

5. Thus spake the seraph; and forthwith
    Appeared a shining throng
   Of angels praising God, who thus
    Addressed their joyful song:

6. 'All glory be to God on high,
    And to the earth be peace;
   Good will henceforth from heaven to men
    Begin and never cease.'

O Little Town of Bethlehem

1. O little town of Bethlehem,
    How still we see thee lie!
   Above thy deep and dreamless sleep
    The silent stars go by:
   Yet in thy dark streets shineth
    The everlasting Light;
   The hopes and fears of all the years
    Are met in thee tonight.

2. For Christ is born of Mary;
    And, gathered all above,
   While mortals sleep, the angels keep
    Their watch of wondering love.
   O, morning stars, together
    Proclaim the holy birth,
   And praises sing to God the King
    And peace to men on earth.

3. How silently, how silently,
    The wondrous gift is given!
   So God imparts to human hearts
    The blessings of his heaven.
   No ear may hear his coming;
    But in this world of sin,
   Where meek souls will receive him, still
    The dear Christ enters in.

4. O holy Child of Bethlehem,
    Descend to us, we pray;
   Cast out our sin, and enter in:
    Be born in us today.
   We hear the Christmas angels
    The great glad tidings tell:
   O come to us, abide with us,
    Our Lord Emmanuel.

We Three Kings

1. We three kings of Orient are;
    Bearing gifts we traverse afar
   Field and fountain, moor and mountain,
    Following yonder star;
   O star of wonder, star of night,
    Star with royal beauty bright,
   Westward leading, still proceeding,
    Guide us to thy perfect light.

2. *Melchior:*
   Born a king on Bethlehem plain,
    Gold I bring, to crown him again –
   King for ever, ceasing never,
    Over us all to reign:
   O star of wonder, etc.

We three kings (cont.)

3. *Caspar:*
   Frankincense to offer have I;
    Incense owns a Deity nigh:
   Prayer and praising, all men raising,
    Worship him, God most high:
   O star of wonder, etc.

4. *Balthazar:*
   Myrrh is mine; its bitter perfume
    Breathes a life of gathering gloom,
   Sorrowing, sighing, bleeding, dying,
    Sealed in the stone-cold tomb:
   O star of wonder, etc.

5. Glorious now, behold him arise;
    King, and God, and sacrifice.
   Heaven sings alleluya,
    Alleluya the earth replies:
   O star of wonder, etc.

Hark! the Herald Angels Sing

1. Hark! the herald angels sing
    Glory to the new-born King,
   Peace on earth and mercy mild,
    God and sinners reconciled.
   Joyful all ye nations rise,
    Join the triumph of the skies;
   With th' angelic host proclaim:
    'Christ is born in Bethlehem'.
   Hark! the herald angels sing
    Glory to the new-born King.

2. Christ, by highest Heav'n adored,
    Christ, the Everlasting Lord,
   Late in time behold him come,
    Offspring of a virgin's womb.
   Veiled in flesh the Godhead see,
    Hail the incarnate Deity!
   Pleased as Man with man to dwell,
    Jesus, our Emmanuel.
   Hark! the herald angels sing
    Glory to the new-born King.

3. Hail, the heaven-born Prince of Peace!
    Hail, the Sun of Righteousness!
   Light and life to all he brings,
    Risen with healing in his wings.
   Mild he lays his glory by,
    Born that man no more may die,
   Born to raise the sons of earth,
    Born to give them second birth.
   Hark! the herald angels sing
    Glory to the new-born King.

Ding Dong Merrily on High

1. Ding dong merrily on high
    In heaven the bells are ringing:
   Ding dong verily the sky
    Is riven with Angel-singing:
   Gloria, Hosanna in excelsis!

2. E'en so here below, below
    Let steeple bells be swungen.
   And io, io, io
    By priest and people sungen:
   Gloria, Hosanna in excelsis!

3. Pray you, dutifully prime
    Your matin chime, ye ringers;
   May you beautifully rime
    Your evetime song, ye singers:
   Gloria, Hosanna in excelsis!

Deck the Hall

1. Deck the hall with boughs of holly,
    Fa la la la la, la la la la,
   'Tis the season to be jolly,
    Fa la la la la, la la la la.
   Don we now our gay apparel,
    Fa la la, la la la, la la la,
   Sing the ancient Yule-tide carol,
    Fa la la la la, la la la la.

2. See the blazing Yule before us,
    Fa la la la la, la la la la,
   Strike the harp and join the chorus,
    Fa la la la la, la la la la.
   Follow me in merry measure,
    Fa la la, la la la, la la la,
   While I tell of Yule-tide treasure,
    Fa la la la la, la la la la.

3. Fast away the old year passes,
    Fa la la la la, la la la la,
   Hail the new, you lads and lasses,
    Fa la la la la, la la la la.
   Sing we joyous all together,
    Fa la la, la la la, la la la,
   Heedless of the wind and weather,
    Fa la la la la, la la la la.

Jingle Bells

Dashing through the snow,
In a one-horse open sleigh,
O'er the fields we go,
Laughing all the way;
Bells on bobtail ring,
Making spirits bright;
What fun it is to ride and sing
A sleighing song tonight.
Jingle bells, jingle bells,
Jingle all the way,
Oh, what fun it is to ride
In a one-horse open sleigh.

See, amid the Winter's Snow

1. See, amid the winter's snow,
   Born for us on earth below,
   See, the tender lamb appears,
   Promised of eternal years.
   Hail, thou ever blessed morn!
   Hail, Redemption's happy dawn!
   Sing through all Jerusalem,
   Christ is born in Bethlehem!

2. Lo, within a manger lies
   He who built the starry skies,
   He who, throned in height sublime,
   Sits amid the cherubim.   *Refrain*

3. Say, you holy shepherds, say,
   What your joyful news today;
   Wherefore have you left your sheep
   On the lonely mountain steep?   *Refrain*

4. "As we watched at dead of night,
   Lo, we saw a wondrous light;
   Angels singing 'Peace on earth'
   Told us of the Saviour's birth."   *Refrain*

5. Sacred infant, all divine,
   What a tender love was thine,
   Thus to come from highest bliss
   Down to such a world as this.   *Refrain*

6. Teach, O teach us, holy child,
   By thy face so meek and mild,
   Teach us to resemble thee
   In thy sweet humility.   *Refrain*

Rocking

1. Little Jesus, sweetly sleep, do not stir,
   We will lend a coat of fur.
   We will rock you, rock you, rock you,
   We will rock you, rock you, rock you,
   See the fur to keep you warm,
   Snugly round your tiny form.

2. Mary's little baby sleep, sweetly sleep,
   Sleep in comfort, slumber deep.
   We will rock you, rock you, rock you,
   We will rock you, rock you, rock you,
   We will serve you all we can,
   Little Jesus, little man.

Text translated by Percy Dearmer, used by permission
of the Oxford University Press.

O Come, All ye Faithful

1. O come, all ye faithful,
      Joyful and triumphant,
   O come ye, O come ye to Bethlehem;
      Come and behold him
   Born the King of angels:
      O come, let us adore him,
      O come, let us adore him,
      O come, let us adore him,
      Christ the Lord.

2. God of God,
      Light of Light,
   Lo, he abhors not the Virgin's womb;
      Very God,
   Begotten not created:
      O come, etc.

3. Sing, choirs of angels,
      Sing in exultation,
   Sing, all ye citizens of heaven above;
      Glory to God
   In the highest:
      O come, etc.

4. Yea, Lord, we greet thee,
      Born this happy morning,
   Jesu, to thee be glory given;
      Word of the Father,
   Now in flesh appearing:
      O come, etc.

We Wish you a Merry Christmas

1. We wish you a merry Christmas,
      We wish you a merry Christmas,
   We wish you a merry Christmas,
      And a happy New Year.
   Good tidings we bring
      To you and your kin;
   We wish you a merry Christmas,
      And a happy New Year.

2. Now bring us some figgy pudding,
      Now bring us some figgy pudding,
   Now bring us some figgy pudding,
      And bring some out here.
   Good tidings, etc.

3. For we all like figgy pudding,
      For we all like figgy pudding,
   For we all like figgy pudding,
      So bring some out here.
   Good tidings, etc.

4. And we won't go until we've had some,
      And we won't go until we've had some,
   And we won't go until we've had some,
      So bring some out here.
   Good tidings, etc.

O Little Town of Bethlehem

American Tune

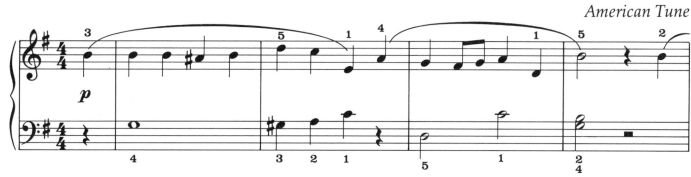

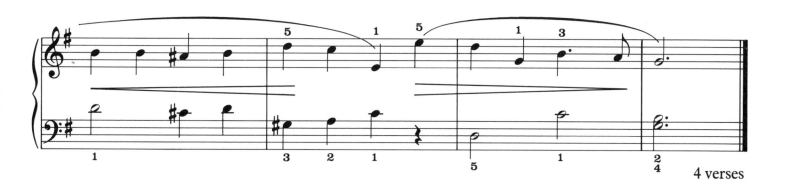

4 verses

We Three Kings

5 verses

Hark! the Herald Angels Sing

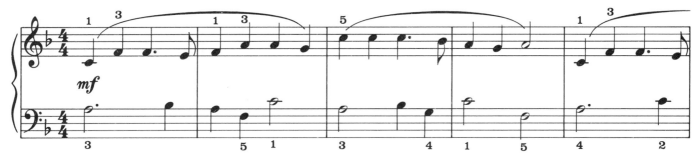

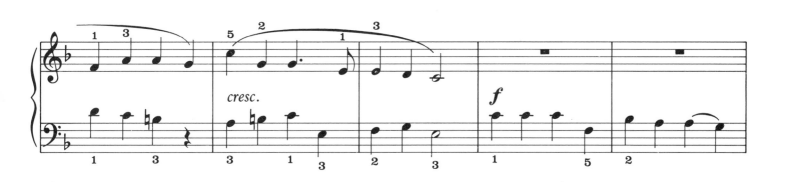

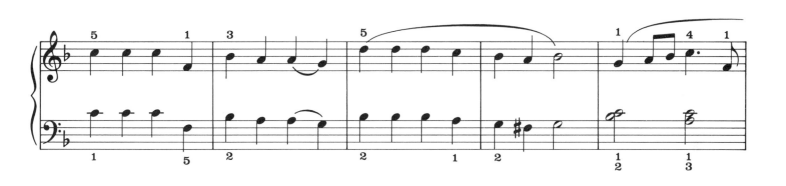

Chorus

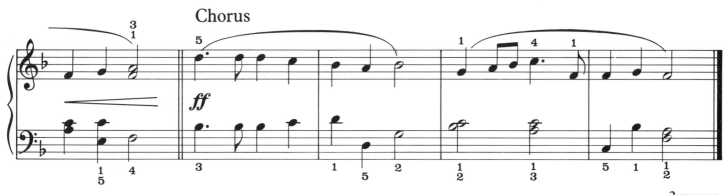

3 verses

Ding Dong Merrily on High

Chorus

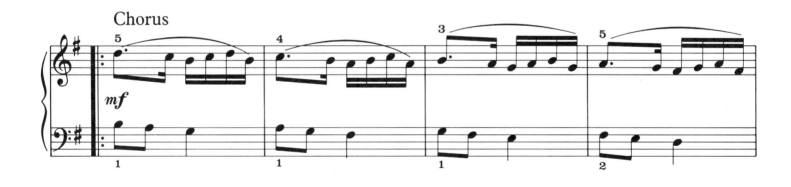

3 verses

Deck the Hall

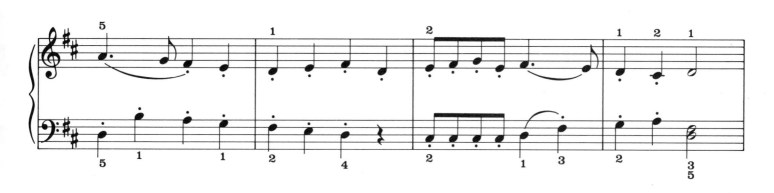

3 verses

Jingle Bells

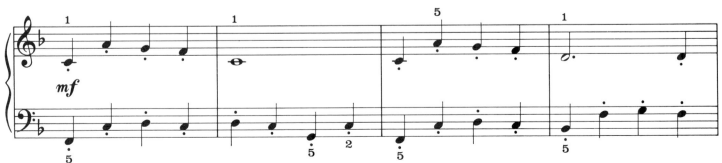

Chorus

See, amid the Winter's Snow

SECONDO

6 verses

See, amid the Winter's Snow

PRIMO

6 verses

Rocking

SECONDO

poco rit.

2 verses

Rocking

PRIMO

Melody collected by Martin Shaw, from the Oxford Book of Carols; used by permission of the Oxford University Press.

2 verses

O Come, All ye Faithful

SECONDO

4 verses

O Come, All ye Faithful

PRIMO

Chorus

4 verses

We Wish you a Merry Christmas

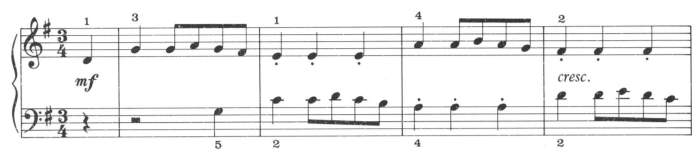

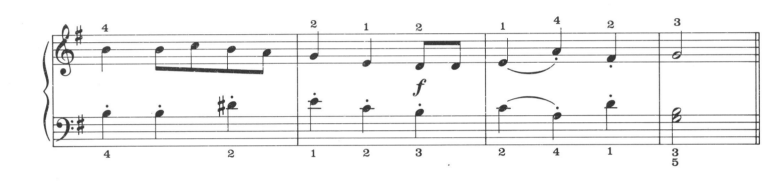

Chorus

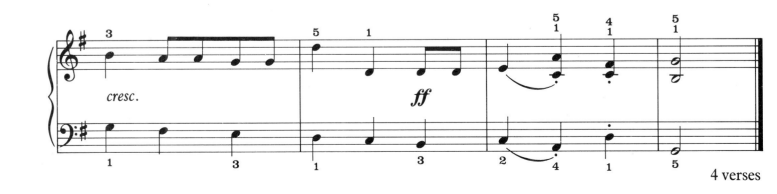

4 verses